HERE

Hannah Martens

BookLeaf
Publishing

India | USA | UK

Presentation by *BookLeaf Publishing*

Web: www.bookleafpub.com

E-mail: info@bookleafpub.com

ISBN: 9789357448741

First edition 2022

DEDICATION

To my little one - I hope you always eat clover
petals

ACKNOWLEDGEMENT

My Great Blessing, David - without you, I never would have given myself this chance

My Mom, featured in "HANDSTITCHED", and my Dad, featured in "YELLOW" - for teaching me what family means before I could even put words together

Rupi Kaur - for transforming thoughts into words in a way that inspires me, and every reader of her works that I've spoken to, to want to write

The Oh Hellos - my poem "Treebark" was fully inspired by a line from the song "There Beneath" on their album 'Dear Wormwood' -
"...I learned that everything (the wind, the leaves)
Has breath inside..."

Victoria Anne D'Anna - it is such a happy thing to see your success as an author bloom and grow. Following your process in the creation of "The Flower that Wouldn't Grow" gave me courage to seek out writing, myself

Every professional involved in our adoption process - for the genuine compassion you have showed to every member of my family, even before we were one

PREFACE

This little collection is for everyone who has been touched by adoption - whether you have lived through adoption in your own life, or are curious about the realities of adoption. For those of you who have walked this path as people who have adopted or as people who have been adopted, I hope these words hold some sort of comfort or meaning for you, in some way. For those who are learning, the highs and lows ahead may be different from what you expected. As I write this, I am at the very beginning of this new level of my life. I am by no means an expert on adoption - and I'm sure that I will spend the rest of my entire life at the beginning. This collection represents the story of my own family, and how mothering has shaped me in the past and now.

Every new day we are reminded through little moments, beautiful or not, to celebrate that our family (like your own) truly is forever. I hope, if nothing else, you might see here that you are not alone - you never have been.

ORIGINS

I have been surrounded by strength my entire
life
and have had strong heaped upon me
I have been moved by it the way water rolls over
stone
until it is a polished marble
it's no wonder I grew up knowing how to
lift up those around me
because if I keep all this strong just for me
I'm no better than the mud at the bottom of the
lake
why would I ever keep all this strong to myself
and how could I

OVERMUCH

In the cockpit,
the pilot sees hundreds of
buttons, switches, dials, knobs
he knows what to do
he can rest easy with
AUTO-PILOT and stay the course
but I've known since I was small
that this is not an aircraft meant for travel -
it is a rocket designed to go out far, far from here
I have no such luxury
I cannot rest
some buttons blink, some alarms sound off
and I am tasked to diffuse them all
the pilot knows, and trusts the plan -
I have too much awareness
to trust anything but my own two hands
they just can't go fast enough, that's all

there's always going to be another flashing
button to deal with
and all I have, is to smash all the right buttons
as this rocket flies forward
and hope to slow
its destruction
and now, I'm getting older -
the pressure of space around me still counts but

the vacuum that pulls is child's play
compared to the demands of the mission
and the breakneck velocity of the rocket itself -

and no,
knowing that I might just be a passenger
does not change a thing

BURSTING AT THE SEAMS

grief is like a suitcase
we all carry with us
but as convenient as that might seem,
the zipper is only so strong
and sometimes,
it's such a full case
that the zipper is pulled too tight
it's these times
that I walk fastest -
not to be rude, or avoid people
but because if I stop moving
the zipper might give
and my grief will spill out all over the floor
I know I can't
leave this suitcase behind -
the contents are too valuable
and even though it is bursting at the seams,
whenever I see something that belongs on the
inside
I reach for it
even though I have no room
and I know that stopping traffic for me is not the
way
but no amount of well-meaning people
can pack it up for me again,
pack it "the right way" to make it fit nicer,

though some try -
I only wish
they would ask my permission
before opening it up and
exposing it to all the people

as days roll on,
the contents settle
the zipper stretches and
the suitcase holds together
but make no mistake -
everything is still in there,
and any bump or jostle
might just -

MY GREAT BLESSING

I have been charmed by the berries,
enchanted by the strength of the leaves
and brought to tears by the color
but the way every part works together as one
captivates and fascinates me
more than anything
the way every green hand loves on everything it
touches
and how the all the parts choose to spend their
life
working together
for better or for worse
how they choose to spend every minute of their
time
embracing the house falling apart beneath
just to show that it is worthy of decades of love
and the way the whole vine covers over all the
worst parts
and leaves a kiss wherever it goes
is my favorite thing
that is its nature
but the most precious part, more than anything
is that every season
the ivy only grows fuller
grows, grows
grows

TREEBARK

some little rough brown patch peeled
lying in the grass
is a form of its own,
more than just the scraps leftover from what was
once
pulled up from the dirt by holy hands
and stretched into a home for all kinds -
that same little rough brown patch
forgotten on the ground has left behind
the grand reveal of a paler, smoother body
just like bone -
longer and farther than arms can reach
that lends more strength and height
than my legs
just like skin -
that decorates the whole tree,
or roots that provide connection,
some little rough brown
grows into its colors by the season and
holds time in wrinkles and rings
just like me -
on the ground
what we have in common with some little rough
is that here in this place, we have the best view
of

swaying shadows and the
underbelly of every crawling thing
that wanders past us
as though we were dust, too,
too little to be minded
but even the dust is teeming with life
everything has breath inside

NESTING

these are two hands
that shook out the echinacea seeds,
during the rainiest days
and kept them safe and warm and dry

that opened doors for the wind
to bring purpose here,
and the windows too, for good measure

that gathered all the thyme and savory
and dried them in the windows
and watched all the people walk by with the
same jealous wish on their tongues

that pulled strawberries every morning,
held onto the freshest peppers every afternoon,
carved open pomegranates every evening
and saved it all to give freely to my little one

these are the hands
that celebrate every new grey hair
that pray thankfulness over these days
for every fallen leaf
and every wayward goose feather and
for every last sigh of warm that knows cold is
hiding around the corner

these hands are mine
and they have worked from one October to the
next
to build a nest that can weather the storms
to prepare for any kind of egg that might hatch
here

PREMOTHER

My hands have always been ready for you
with open fingers and
veins glowing through in
soft blues and violets
though I still reach for wisdom,
all I have gathered is yours
I hope you'll always look to find calm here
and let me give what I have to you
and let me bless you with everything I've got

HANDSTITCHED

Your gifts are handstitched with
care and precision and
prayers and blessings
and wishes for good
and all these precious things, you give away -
after all the time and effort, you have kept no
pieces for yourself
yet you keep lavishing people with your best
hopes
you keep making
and giving and giving
and giving

I wish my loved ones
could wear my heart around, too
wrap themselves in my very own handmade love
but even with your mittens and hats
my fingers are too frantic
my head is too windy
and I know, no matter what I do, that
no amount of practice or skill
can even come close to the gifts you've given to
me

Maybe the reason you're so driven
to wake up and stitch your love into gifts, is
because
your children were
hemmed and sewn together
inside of you
and even after they were born
the love was too much -
so no matter how much you give away
it just keeps growing

ANIMAL

I learned as a child,
the soul lies somewhere in the body
but keen eyes can find mine
on the outside
old, but tireless
peeking through crows feet and
scrunching my worry lines
warming my lips and
flexing the fingers
pouring pink all over me and
splashing into the corner of my eyes
holding word and breath and thought
at all the wrong times
an impulsive, feral creature
with enough feeling to be a
being of its own
full of life and ready for anything
keen eyes can catch a glimpse, plainly enough
scurrying through the underbrush,
dodging shadows and
making little homes along the way
and now that my role in this world is on the edge
of changing forever,
the thing cannot sit still

ABUNDANCE

it astonishes me
that we are just days away from
a whole little person to pour love into
brimming with ideas
claiming us with new names
running through our doors
my whole body feels this blessing
I pray that I never lose sight of the treasure in
coming home to stay

YELLOW

the first thing I remember
is standing on a yellow slide
with yellow leaves falling fast all around me
as far as I could see
and you were standing at the bottom
with open arms reaching up
saying "I'll catch you" -
this memory, my very first one
has set the tone
for the rest of my entire life
because even though I don't remember coming down
I know that you never let me fall -
I know that you've never let me hit the ground
and that you are still reaching to comfort me
even now that I am standing at the bottom
earning the trust of my own little one

CLOVERFLOWER

I know I am profoundly blessed
that I get to be the one
to hold back laughter
while your tiny fist holds tight on a clover stem
and you pinch your chubby fingers around the
petals of the flower,
pluck them with all your might, and
chew them up
as if eating the purple clover petals will turn you
purple, yourself

trust me when I tell you that
I count every today as the most wonderful one,
yet
and that I could never be full of your voice
trying to get my attention

"MAMA"

you have all of my attention already, my silly
one
you don't even need to call for me
my ears are at the ready
I can't take my mind off of you, much less my
heart, much less my eyes

and as happy as we are, even on the happiest
days
as delighted as I am that I get to be here with
you
I still remember that my role has been filled,
before
even when we are laughing to the point of tears
I will never forsake the importance of watching
your small moments
like learning to munch on clover petals

OUR KIND

in the smudges on the windows,
my eyes read the words
"welcome home"
and I know that even if I
open the door
and find that I am the only one here,
I am still surrounded by all the love
I've ever felt
and all that's on the way

MADCAP

How such a young person
can carry a whole volcano in your chest
shakes my whole head
all the heavy of the past is a weight that I can not
carry for you
but I wish with everything I have that I could

we may never have all the pieces
but I'll fill in the blanks while I'm able
to stitch some peace together for you as well as I
can

VOW

I see that the struggle to gain control
over things that are beyond your power
comes from a lack of trust in the things that
should have been trustworthy
comes from memorizing the pattern of losing
things you trusted
to things you couldn't see
and having no effect on when - or even whether
- the changes happened,
no matter how loud you screamed

I promise
that history will not repeat itself, on my watch
we have so much to learn
but you can rest in the knowledge that you have
a say in all of it, from now on
even if you can't trust the idea just yet

I haven't walked your miles
I cannot truly understand the grief you've carried
on your head
but you can trust me, little one
when I say that I will hold your hand when we
go walking
and make sure the way is safe ahead of us

I have learned firsthand, in my own time, how
grief must be carried everywhere
I don't know where your grief will lead you
but we can go there together
I will walk alongside you, every step
I will be right here

WOODGRAIN

when you scrunched your fingers together all
small
into the best shape you could
and said "i love you with my whole heart too,
mama"
I melted into the grain of the floor
my mind lives here, now
I will be stuck in this room, in this light, for the
rest of my days

BUSHFIRE

in the beginning your fires were blazing
absolutely raging
out of control
it took everything you had
to allow yourself
to accept even a drop of water

you may as well have come home to us with a
box of matches hidden in your pocket

and I am truly, so amazed
that even with hands so small,
you're learning to tame those blazes into cozy
smolders
you don't need so much heat, anymore
just enough to make warm and call it a day
my hope is that someday soon
the warm of laughing on the couch and hugging
us at night will fill your heart enough
to put out what's left of the fire you used to rely
on

if we had only known that
trauma is a bushfire
eating and blackening everything it can -

if only we could have prepared ourselves better
fireproofed it all for you
but we did our best
we always have and we always will

we have always known that the fire was
necessary
it just took some time and patience for all of it
to burn down, and for the wind to blow the ash
away
just look at us, now
together is a better kind of beauty

ROCKET

my little one curled up in my arms yawning
while the sun went down
and gently promised me
"when I get bigger, we can go to the moon and
sit there"
but look around -
you've already brought us to the moon
here we are
so high above the ground
that we can scoop this happy dream right up in
our hands

GLOWING

my head is dripping with favor

wealth
prosperity
peace
fertility

but the abundance of
blessing over me
is so much more than meets the eye

my wealth is in memory
my prosperity is in affection
my peace is in the garden
and even though I never carried my baby inside
of me, fertility fountains from my hands

HOME

you may find me resting in
a ribbon of smoke
swirling around inside the glass jar,
and the bite of the cinnamon
that lives in every mother's spice cupboard

my hearth is in between the stones
we laid with our bare hands -
I gather the sticks and twigs for
the fire that we make
every night, all seasons
and I am the warmest one

I am the one who
chose the magnolia trees,
carried wood for the fence,
spread quail's egg over the walls -
and the scratches on the floor
we laid on hands and knees in the kitchen,
that is where I sign my name
over every meal

this place is filled with all the finest sounds
my ears ever heard
whistling trains in the distance
sizzling meat in the next room over

wind in the trees
clumsy piano keys
and now, the footsteps of my little one

my home is wherever my footprints lead and
wherever I laugh after the sun has tucked itself
in under the fields
wherever I am, wherever I make it to

I have spent my life building it from
countless bits and pieces of
what matters most to me
throw a log on the fire and
find welcome wherever you may

SPIRITED

I've been treating my mind like a ghost
that wails like a siren,
sends warnings and shows up in unexpected
places
I have run along the edge of
fear and understanding
but I know that I am not haunted
my mind is not a ghost at all
it's just a wild thing
jumping home through the trees after dark
and now, it is time to enjoy the harvest of peace
that we've worked for
and have faith that all is well, and that morning
is about here
everything I've ever been and done before now,
is sealed up for good -
maybe when I am old, I'll have time to retrieve it
in bits and pieces
but for now, I will stop chasing these young days
running away from me
and hold your hand while we chase yours
the sun is rising
and I'm so glad you're here

www.ingramcontent.com/pod-product-compliance
Lightning Source LLC
La Vergne TN
LVHW010934200726
843509LV00013B/2222